Gracious
Is the
Earth

Mark Christhilf

TO SOW THE FALLOW SOIL

Winston-Derek Publishers, Inc.
Pennywell Drive—P.O. Box 90883
Nashville, TN 37209

First printing

PUBLISHED BY WINSTON-DEREK PUBLISHERS, INC.
Nashville, Tennessee 37205

Library of Congress Catalog Card No: 90-83592
ISBN: 1-55523-376-7

Printed in the United States of America

Contents

Acknowledgements

Some of the poems have appeared or will soon be published in the following periodicals:

"Montezuma," *Roanoke Review* (forthcoming)

"Handshaking," *Modern Age* (forthcoming)

"Tale of the Hands," *North Dakota Quarterly* 57 (Summer 1989)

"The Sentence," "Town Crier," "The Ladder," *High Plains Literary Review* 4 (Spring 1989)

"Letter From Illinois," *Midwest Quarterly* 30 (Winter 1989)

"Ocean," *Kansas Quarterly* 20 (Summer 1988)

"Flowers," *Midwest Quarterly* 29 (Spring 1988)

"Prairies," *Mississippi Valley Review* 17 (Spring 1988)

"The Garden," *Roanoke Review* 14 (Winter 1988)

"Lines," *Kansas Quarterly* 19 (Summer 1987)

"Wave," *Kansas Quarterly* 19 (Winter/Spring, 1987)

"Elder," "Nobody," *The South Dakota Review* 24 (Summer 1986)

"Mountains," *The Pennsylvania Review* 2 (Fall/Winter, 1986)

"The Hard Part," *The Yale Literary Magazine* 151, No. 2 (1986)

"For Isaac," *Roanoke Review* 12 (Summer 1985)

"Camel Men," *Karamu* 9 (Fall 1984)

"If Only," *Dryad* Nos. 14 and 15 (Winter 1977)

For Isaac

I

Years later you would ask about the face
That each morning lured him from the house,
And learn with surprise that there was no face,
Nor anything human, except for a voice,
Making each day the same promise.
Years later you came to believe his tale,
Imagining the voice speaking from the hills,
From the darkened cave into which he retired,
Where clothed in stillness and devoid of desire,
He cupped his ears and waited for the whisper.
When he spoke of the voice, it seemed comforting,
For it revealed what would come,
What was more sure than dying,
And through it he lived as in a kind of future,
And never had to wait to understand.
In time the voice led him to seem resolute,
And others recognized that what he knew came true.

II

Years later you remember your mother asking,
One day as he set his face against the morning,
How he could turn his back on you—a son
From his loins, whose immanence enlivened the dawn.
Crossing the room, she held you up to him,
Crying out your need to be touched, and asking
Whether it was wrong for joy to spawn an image,
For surely this was the world, she declared,
And he had coupled with it, fathering this child.
She added that every day through his departure
He closed his eyes to his reflection in the flesh.
Angry, he admitted that in you he took pleasure,

But suddenly cried out that he was not Narcissus,
To be peeping, captivated, at himself all day,
When in life there is love beyond all motion,
Beyond all turning of fathers into sons,
Beyond day and night and their succession.

III

Years later you remember the days he stayed:
All morning about the house together you played.
In the afternoons he carried you to your bed,
And lay you down to sleep a child's sleep.
Attentive, he would bring down his dark face
To cover yours with shaggy beard and breath,
And he locked eyes against yours so deeply lit,
You could see the moving world in their depth.
But when he saw his own face in your eyes,
He grew distant and tenderly stroked you,
And braided your hair back from your brow,
As if he were braiding your thoughts, rehearsing
A time in the future he would take you with him
For a three-day journey onto a mountain
Where again he would tenderly lay you down,
Preparing the act which he heard the voice command,
And which from blind hope he began.

Lines

(for George Panichas)

You forget what plow has carved them.
When these furrows were formed you felt no pain,
Nor was the plowman seen. But if called upon
To recollect long-ago lessons, you could say
What lines reveal in nature's skin.
By circular lines the age of wood is gauged,
And concentric waves register disrupture
On the smooth surface of any water: one stone
Flung into a still pond makes a pattern
Of lines spreading outward from the center.

But the human brow must be another matter.
Those lines on your forehead are not full circles,
But half-moons printed in the skin—by what?
Time's measure? Haste and pressure?
How then have others of your age not been scarred?
A peculiar lesson your wrinkles must spell,
Etching the frown you formed for a lifetime
Against distraction—desire, noise, hunger—
As you pondered the record of human aspiration
With intensity that seared the skin from inside.

Having frowned into focus innumerable books,
Your face is a chart of concentration.
It maps your effort to discover invisible lines—
Directions to be followed through life.
Pleading the value of persistent contemplation,
Your mask is permanent: the lines will not unravel.
Though smoothed at night by sleep, when you awaken
They bunch to life, as if they remember
The wive's tale that we recited as children: who draws
His face into a grimace will have it frozen that way.

Inside you are lined with concern for others,
And do not notice as the lines in your mask thicken.
Arched out between the temples
They form the sturdy net that you cast
By day, hoping to catch the human essence.
It makes me wonder, so I go back to wood and water,
For through this net of lines I glimpse a child,
Standing on a shore in green summer, urged by his will
To cast still farther, toward the lake's center,
The stone that made these lines spread outward.

The Sentence

Cast on everyone for the crime of being born,
This sentence can never be overturned,
And lest anyone forget, it's written in flesh,
Numbering days which must be done.
As the number falls toward the zero point,
The sentence in the skin grows prominent
Until what it says is utterly clear:
The loved flesh is doomed to disappear.

I have seen the flesh of my kin,
Faces of grandfather, mother, cousin,
Vanish with a broken call into the air—
When I look, no one is there.
When I look again, my face is less clear,
In the glass the flesh is faded and sere,
Broken up with fissures and falling down
To show the bones it is hung upon.

The question I've come to dwell upon
Is how should I do my time,
For I'd do more than cringe with fear,
Shrinking from the day I'll not be here.
Reform could be the object of the sentence
If the fading flesh leaves the wits strong
So they can grasp the worth of every day,
Praising it while it passes away.

The Prairies

Do not be disgusted or cringe at their plight.
Their desolation is natural: a tyrannical sky
Presses them flat, demanding that they lie
Prostrate before its overwhelming gaze.
And never will you see them hump or heave
So utter is their fealty: in one plane
Stretching out, they unfold into distance,
Meeting the sky to form the level horizon,
And this unbroken line is their sole resistance,
By which they distinguish themselves from heaven.
Dark and earthy, the line is the reminder
Of the point prairies can be pressed no farther.

Do not be disgusted when they cannot hold the line,
For in winter the sky grows more unkind,
And adds the weight of snow to their burden,
Burying them beneath a huge white ocean.
Transfigured by the whiteness, they give in
And the sky's face glares through the line,
Making them reflect its tone, whether blue or bone,
And you will be unable to tell one from the other,
So much does the world seem one color.
In pure subjection they forget they are prairies,
But do not be disgusted: instead why not say
They reach perfection by giving themselves away.

Flowers

When the face opens toward you above a soft throat,
And from the pink tongue sweet odors come,
You will not wonder that for centuries
Girls were named for them—Camille and Rosemary.
But you will miss the truth of their existence
If duped by the flowery conceits
In which girls and flowers are ornaments,
Cultivated lives from someone's garden,
Watered and protected until the faces blossom,
To bedeck with freshness human occasions:
A wedding's flower girl does lend innocence a face
And a lily near a coffin makes death less sombre,
But such customs hide the flower of the matter.

When her face opens up it has its own occasion,
And noiselessly invades through the eyes
To explode like a bomb on fields of blood within,
Searing and scarring them with a dark reflection
Until the stunned blood falls under its command.
Then beneath the civil skin rioting begins
As the fresh face displaces gods and pets
And instructs blood to forget laws of ownership,
Which were made to prevent its being picked:
In beauty's universal law, flowers and girls,
Like stars burning in the night fields,
Cry forget-me-not, compelling attention
And the desire which insures the generations.

The Ladder

The rule exists for everyone: *ascend.*
True, it is wearing to climb and climb
Toward an unknown height, one rung at a time,
One foot, then another, till the rungs blur
And you forget you are climbing a ladder.
True, there is another direction: some take it,
Although most stop after climbing a bit,
And clinging to one rung, forget ascent,
And claim in heights there is no justice.
These smile and join voices with fatigue,
To praise their station, the view from there,
But this is precisely when to lift your arm,
Grasp the next rung with the hand's palm,
Lift your leg till the foot snags a higher place,
Swing up with the breath of rising on your face,
And feel the muscles stiffen your thigh
As another view welcomes your eye.

Camel Men

As we remember we had always been on route,
Always on a journey from city to city,
And then the act of power was as solid as our trade,
As we bartered with caravans of spice and grain,
Though we dreamed of travel without possessions
And of motion in a feathery air.

That we had once been chieftains no one doubted,
Even sands that will never welcome us
Shifted for our singular path and purpose
And the dark eyes in the hovels
Shone to mirror our success
Though our riches now are bones in the desert.

And the subjects who attended us
Believed in their small concessions,
And in their bias our status was.
Each summer their talismen chased off locusts
As they made us gods of commerce
And gave themselves like a hungering mouth.

Until on one journey the unforgotten need
Welled up like darkness in one of us
And at night, far from the next oasis,
Between sleep and waking in his own tent,
He seemed to see the shadow of his huge beast
Obtruding slowly onto the firelit canvas wall.

Outside the cold seemed to snap and sparkle
And the barren distance made him feel he dreamed.
At first it was only the head of his camel
Silhouetted on the tent wall in a gesture
Like a threat except it caused no alarm
For the cold it was goaded all dumb brutes.

So he had allowed it as he told us later,
The beast itself was a pledge of trust
Among our people and though harsh

9

And hateful on the mornings of departure
They carried their own water in a twin hump
And the shaggy hides made a warm cover.

Therefore the head was tolerated and the long neck,
But the sound it made breathing began to disturb him,
So when the shoulders pushed inside
He pondered the ingratitude
And lying there warm as he deserved
The rude response of all of them in all time.

And when the shaggy beast had finally come inside,
And the musk smell crawled on the walls of the tent,
Its weight and presence mounted to a challenge
And he had risen quietly, seizing his spear,
Driving the glittering shaft honed from good metal
Full into the chest of the useful animal.

Now because of this we wander,
And following him have sworn off camels
With the baggage and belief they require,
And follow the stars across the deserts
On horseback and with no tents,
Though they still know us as camel men.

Around fires late at night we commemorate,
Telling the story over and over,
Preserving a legend that no book speaks,
And by the clean intelligence we make our vows,
For though we now drink the water of cactuses,
The slow beasts of burden no longer limit speed.

Now we hunt, secure in our memory,
Though at times our transient lot seems frightful
In desert solitude without towns for destination.
We subsist on small game less swift than our intent.
We flush it toward the opening plains of sand
And pursue it with full measure of our lore.

At the Grave of a Friend

Back again, aren't you? And you're not sure why,
After all, it's clear what I've become:
Upright stone, two dates and a name,
Presiding over a vacant plot.
But it's what happens to all of us,
You knew that when we were friends.
There's something else you've been considering
Since the day you helped lay me in the ground.

Let me see if I can help you a bit.
Weren't you always impressed by my voice?
By the way it seemed to begin down deep
Beyond my lungs, in an unknown place,
Then swelling with a solemn rise and fall,
It cast a kind of spell upon the ears.
But it was mine, wasn't it, and mine alone,
Marking me more surely than my name.

Am I right so far? And weren't you impressed
By the justice of everything I said?
Didn't my voice seem to make you more real,
Describing the path which you were on—
Not in the words you might have used,
But from the viewpoint of everyone?
And when you expected too much from others,
It would mention our brief stay here.

How did I come by it? Isn't that next?
Well, that part is hardest to explain.
From what I remember it was years and years
Before the voice gained a life of its own
From the strife between a notion of myself
And the man I was, with groping eyes and hands.
You know the one I mean, who bears us down,
So that *no* to him is *yes* to the notion.

And now you want me to go on, don't you,
And tell you whether it meant anything,
Whether, from where I am, it was worth it
To treat the creature in me with disdain.
All I can tell you is to look at yourself,
Sitting on a tombstone, head bent down,
With eyes half-closed, ears open for a clue.
You hear me right now, don't you?

Handshaking

After years of practicing with friends,
The shaking habit which elders began,
It held me so hard in its hand,
I'm amazed that its grip loosened.
But one gathering made me feel
The hands weren't pressing goodwill,
For one palm just suffered my grip,
And one uneasy about friendship
Grasped fast and released too quick.
At last a hard palm wrung my hand
With what seemed a challenge,
So I thought shaking had no purpose
And planned greetings which kept distance:
A nod or a brief word with lips
Seemed more refined than pressing flesh,
And would give time a hand with friendship.

Without the habit nothing seemed wrong,
Until my job put me beside a man.
Usual in looks and disposition,
Except for his shaking habit.
Although I spoke, I made no motion,
But daily he made show of welcome,
By turning trunk, extending hand,
And pumping mine up and down.
Then in time my liking deepened,
Until at work I'd wait for him,
And if he missed for some reason,
I felt a vague dejection.
Now thinking back through time on him,
I see his shake was the connection,
For goodwill was a ghost in me,
Until shaking gave it a body.

Town Crier

I'd rather be the crier than the cooper,
Rather cry than be the hatter:
Commanding hands, with brows bent down,
Those others shaped the boards or furs
Into goods for the people in town,
But labored, they did, without words.

I'd rather be the crier than the pastor,
Although the pastor did use words:
All week he planned a Sunday lecture
About the need for a Christian manner,
But this idea, preached week by week,
Put many townspeople to sleep.

The judge, too, he pondered words,
But still I'd be the crier:
Lives often hung on the judge's ruling,
But he used laws handed down,
So for people with good schooling,
His words were well foreknown.

But when the crier walked the town,
His words sounded like alarms:
Crashing through the walls of homes,
They roused ears straight from boredom,
And eyes all widened wondering
Just how town life would change.

Theme with Variations

I

I think we do not much like looking up
For the vault surges, deep and inhuman,
And the vapors drift, forming, falling, reforming,
To remind us of the time before our time.
Far beyond are the stars, the countless
Billions, in galaxies, unnamed and unseen:
Stars which once provided sure directions,
Which now move, on all sides, away from us,
Departing at speeds which are numbing to the mind
Into the dark where boundaries are unknown.

I think we do not much like looking up,
For just overhead the ideas are waiting.
Voiceless, patient, invisible as gods,
Each unexhausted by the way it is known,
By the centuries of names, terms, languages:
The perfect man being Moses, Christ, Mohammed.
They wait indifferently, no respecter of persons,
In fact, they ask for self-forgetfulness.
To receive them is to suffer their consequences—
Discomfort to the flesh, frustration of acts.

And yet the ideas are all that is left
And can make us feel strangely complete.

II

What are the mathematicians naming
When they conceive a point where motion ends;
And write it as a number which has no worth,
Using the zero, borrowed from Hindu priests?
What are they doing, adding zero to the sums,
And showing it unchanged after division?

15

They are naming nothing: inventing terms
For infinities of distance and time;
Infinities which can bend a beam of light,
Bend the longest and fastest of straight lines,
Until it arcs and returns like a boomerang,
To form a zero, to measure nothing.

They are taming the unknown with terms,
Naming an idea Greek sages called the *One*;
And the Indians, *Wakonda*, and the Christians, *God*.
Naming the zero-zone of darkness, gas, and dust
Out of which the light-giving stars once spun;
And toward which they now are burning, dying down.

They are naming nothing, a place without time,
Where the beginning and the end are one;
Where the round gate between the woman's thighs
Is the grave, the waiting, opened ground:
A dark hole, unmoving, exuding depth,
Forming a zero-point for all the days and works.

III

The tale is never told. Remember that.
So did Rousseau name man a noble savage
After hearing of an Indian brought to London,
Who was unmoved by luxuries of modern life
And longed to return to his homeland.
He named the savage noble, having never seen
New World altars where the Aztec priests
Tied down brethren, and cut out their hearts,
Cut the hearts from terror-stricken, heaving chests,
And boiled them in silver chafing dishes.

The tale is never told. So did Marx name
The perfect state a Communism. After reading
Rousseau's writings in a smoky London flat,
He saw each person bowing to a collective
Will: "Giving according to his capacity,
Receiving according to his need." He named
Without grasping the dark source of freedom
In the *Ungrund*—countless possible being—
Which calls each one to determine his existence
And reminds him that he will die alone.

The tale is never told. So did Mother Church
Dress the nymphs Greeks imagined in woodlands.
She robed the forms singing naked in the streams,
Fixed wings to shoulder blades, named them angels,
And paid Bernini to set them in stone.
Now modern producers have undressed them again,
Parading long limbs and luminous flesh
Across huge screens for the pleasure of the masses.
And renaming them starlets and movie queens,
They describe the mythic lives in magazines.

Three names for one form, made of perfect lines,
Drawn upon imagination: all sigh sweetly
Of their beginning in a place, or a time,
Which is not unlike heaven. There youth,
There tenderness go on and on, as if
May and June should continue all year long.
The question is not whether one name or tale
Is correct, but whether the theme, like all ideas,
Concerns perfection, concerns a good requiring action.
Yet no one learns the answer until the end.

Montezuma

He got no answer, no matter how many hearts
He boiled in the silver chafing dishes.
No voice from heaven fell upon his ears
As he lay listening in his darkened rooms.
He got no answer from the face which stared
From cotton hangings painted by his artists—
The face which led the people who had come,
Like the future, to the shores of his nation.
Were the high pale forehead and bearded lips
Announcing fulfillment of a promise
In which lions lie together with lambs
And the people of all countries live as one?
Or was it just a face, foreign, different,
Yet no better than his own? Messengers
Reported how desire crossed its features
When it saw his gifts of women and gold.
And if the face were ruled by a corrupt heart,
What good were the marvels—the wheel, the iron,
The fierce deer which pulled any burden?
He got no answer, and walking to the window,
Looked out across the city he loved,
The city of cities, with markets where vendors
Sold turquoise bracelets and feather dresses.
A word to his warriors might be its preservation,
Instead he heard his voice command a welcome.
And even later, while being stoned by his people,
He didn't know whether weakness moved his tongue,
Or whether strength lay in embracing change.

The Loyalists

We know what we'd have done—embraced change,
Risked our homes and the welfare of the children—
And think with scorn on these hidebound colonists,
Taking tea as they awaited the ships,
Which brought comforts and letters from kinsmen.
We know what we'd have done, and shrug away
The thought of what they later suffered,
Beating streets in Montreal and Halifax,
Or brooding over losses on Nassau's beach.
Even those whom neighbors tarred and feathered,
Fail to inspire more than brief concern,
For they made their choices without imagination.

We know what we'd have done—until the time
An expert declares we should suppress
A habit we always thought becoming—
And we resist, moving closer to them.
Then suddenly mother, dad, or spouse,
Grows despotic, making foolish demands,
And we're surprised to find we go along,
Recalling how often in the past they helped.
Refusing anger, we simply go along
And hope that tomorrow they'll be themselves.
But now we know it can be hard to fathom
Where freedom starts and loyalty ends.

Letter from Illinois

Morris Birkbeck, original settler in Illinois,
How did you see the prairie as a home?
Settlers before you came to the same ground,
Saw only grasses taller than a man,
Bent to waves by breezes, blossoming with flies,
Unfolding as if endless in a single plane:
Without a rise the prairies joined the skies
And coiled around in an unbroken line,
The same whichever way they turned.
Accustomed to resting upon a rise of hills
And to intrigue of densely growing woods,
Their eyes wearied of the flat expanse;
And fearful to find not a ridge for cover,
Most settlers turned back or passed over.

But in virgin emptiness you saw something more:
Having crossed seas from England at age fifty-four,
You travelled westward through Ohio's hills,
And set your eyes upon the challenge of the fields.
Roaming to the skyline, then back again,
Surveying, measuring, filling it all in,
They partitioned the fluid seas of grass,
Erecting farms to float upon each tract,
Building the clusters of barns and bins,
And digging wells to water hogs and lambs.
Then your eyes struck rich soil beneath,
And guessing it would support a useful grass,
Stretched out the miles of tasseled corn,
Which would feed the generations.

Copperheads

When you hear their name a bell will ring,
And you'll remember they are not pit vipers,
But do you think crooked the many thousands
Whom even the Great Emancipator
Could not persuade to wear blue or bear arms?
Nor did the Stars and Bars inspire them,
Despite the theories of the Civil War buffs;
Instead, on farms from Illinois to Maryland,
And all the way northward into New York,
These plowed the fields and planted the corn
While great groans circled in the neighboring air
And never once fell upon their ears.

They couldn't figure what the fighting was for,
Why old friends from surrounding farms
All of a sudden soured on peace and order,
And with guns took opposing positions.
And when they saw the same friends, back from war,
Sitting round the town square in uniforms,
They heard the bitter taunts, but couldn't figure
Why things had to change from what they were.
Even the thought of one man owning another
Was not enough to stir them to anger.
Surely it was no cause to risk life and limb
For, after all, they had their freedom.

River Town with a Ferry

Progress, whatever were you doing
When you changed your direction,
Leaving this town with no bridge
To join the river's shorelines.
For centuries you coursed these banks,
And settlers called you river-names,
For every one of them felt thanks
To watch you sliding over plains.
At a good speed for your time,
You brought the barges laden down—
Not just with whiskey, hogs, or grain—
But with new settlers from upstream.

Then you wheeled inland with new tastes
For steel rails and concrete,
And drew most people in your wake,
Settling them on new town streets.
But others would not budge one bit
And stayed to work the barge traffic,
Or else to fish the channel cats
For sale to nearby fish markets:
The river's rising, falling time
Convinces them that you went wrong,
And their eyes now stare with scorn
At travelers in your direction.

The Trucker

Suggest that he doesn't know where he's going
And a fist might land in your face.
Hasn't his life followed the highway line,
Unwinding and bending between two coasts,
Followed it to New York, Fort Worth, San Fran,
And once there, hasn't he steered north or west,
Wheeling freight to an exact street address?

Suggest that he doesn't know where he's going,
And at the least you will get a gruff lecture
About how trucks are the nation's lifeline,
Out-hauling trains ever since the Great War.
They've carried everything you wear or own.
Why, even the chair on which you're parked,
Once travelled the highway in a truck.

Suggest that he can't know where he's going
Without knowing where he's been. As he grows
Of Texas or the hills of Maryland,
The bluster, the shaggy beard, the scowl,
The unusual girth of the man in his jeans,
Cinched by scrolled belt with shiny buckle,
Will bring to your mind the river men.

His kin, these steered arks and broadhorns,
Down the nation's first watery highways—
Down Ohio, Wabash, and Cumberland.
His kin, their youthful spirits groaned
To sit in the schoolrooms reading book-lines:
This is the breed which grows restless in town
And chooses a life full of motion.

Al

Thirty-six hours! Just look at it burn!
They won't be calling me strange anymore.
J. P. and the rest have got to respect
An inventor who can bottle light.
Thirty-six hours! After twenty long months,
With nature trying to make me look the fool,
Hiding the secret of a perfect filament,
While I tested platinum, cork, and twine,
Even some hairs from old MacKensie's beard
I carboned and baked in the furnace downstairs
Before that cotton thread holds the current.
Twenty long months! It's because she's mixed up,
Air with fire, gold, and iron with granite—
You've got to divide her into her parts,
Recombine them and watch her react . . .
But the light was different. What strange stuff!
It wants to show everything but itself,
And it's hard to grasp the thing on which seeing
Depends. Now I know why Heraclitus
Called it the being of being, and why the Nazarene
Cast himself as the way, the truth, and the light.
There were times I felt like him, sitting here
Alone all night, staring at the wall
While gaslights fumed, while the doubters slept!
Now that's behind me! It's my name
Which will echo from millions of tongues.
It's my lamp which will transform the world,
All night the streets will be free of crime—
But what pleases most is in every home
After dark in living rooms, families
Will gather . . . mother and father together,
While youngsters, relieved of chores and burdens,
Will be reading their Gibbon and Hume. . . .

24

Thirty-eight hours! Now the sky's the limit!
I'm going to bottle life! I'll begin
With a talking machine—capturing the voice.
Speech now moves in wires across the ocean,
Wouldn't it move a part in a machine
Which would press a disk on a turning drum,
So the sound kind of sets itself down?
After that trick, I'll attach the machine
To a camera which captures motion.
Eastman said he could make special film,
What I'll need to do is invent a shutter
To open and close forty times a second
And break a movement up into fractions.
Then we'll pass these frames before a viewer
And it will seem one continuous action!
Motion and sound! It'll beat the Panoramas!
It'll make the old Wheel of Life look sick!
Why, in great houses across the country
People will think of me as they marvel
At stagings of Lear, Macbeth, and Hamlet,
At the operas of Verdi and Rossini.
And the home will have another blessing
Since my phonograph will serve by itself
To bring smack into the living rooms
The melodies of Mozart and Beethoven.
There's nothing so uplifting as good music,
And what's more, it binds the generations,
I can see parents playing for their children
The same songs they learned when young . . .
The boys at the lab are still skeptical,
Thinking what if people use the machines
To bottle base life—nonsense or rape—
But who'd think of doing a thing like that?

The Magic Window

Everyone tells me to get my eyes checked
When they hear that I can't see the magic.
But, I'm tired of watching the cops and robbers,
The rippers, the rapers, the dark drug plots,
The high speed chases, the inevitable justice
Served by heroes with perennial good looks.

Everyone says I'm being too logical,
But I'm tired of people flying through the air,
Of the long-buried dead returning to life,
Of goblins with feelings, of people possessed.
I'm tired of laughter at another's expense,
Urged by showmen with smug little grins.

Most of all I'm tired of people screaming
At a rate which makes the mind spin,
About how to clean the teeth, skin, breath—
About the secrets of perpetual youth.
I'm tired of hearing what to eat and when,
About laxatives to treat the other end.

Everyone says I'm too cynical
When I blame it on the poets and producers
Who rehash the farces and ancient myths
And base Edenic archetypes on wealth.
It's simple stuff to keep the mind enrapt,
While the boss pitches goods from the market.

Just once I'd like to watch a movie or show
And see myself in the mirroring screen,
See a person swimming in the depths of life.
I'd like a tale of lost causes, undoable mistakes,
Or one about the work required by success—
Something to give the brain a little kick.

Oh Walt Disney, poet of the multitude,
Through the window your images grew real,
Until you created entire worlds to house them
On Orlando's acres and in Anaheim.
Now each day thousands of children of all ages
Board turbo jets, and flock there for a visit.
After being greeted by a smiling duck,
They see the frontiers of their nation's past,
See beneath the oceans and out into space,
Learn how life is lived in China and Japan,
In Mexico, Morocco, Canada, and Norway.
They see them all in a single day!
Walt Disney, successor to Walt Whitman,
Winner of thirty Academy Awards,
Your cartoon worlds now employ forty thousand,
And each year, forty million come,
While the stock in your company outsells U.S. Steel,
And its net worth approaches five billion.

Newscast

I'd learned it's important to be informed,
So every night I turned on the news,
But by the time it ended I'd feel bored,
As if I'd heard the program before.
Then one night a voice came on the air
From some station (or maybe from within);
It changed my understanding of what news is,
And I recall exactly what it said:

"Item One: The Race is perpetually run
For a cup, a title, or a pennant,
By the fleetest, strongest men and women,
And every city fields its teams.
To the average mortal, athletes are gods,
For they can slip the grasp of Time and Space,
So long after Greeks crowned Olympic champs,
It's news when the Braves beat the Giants.

"Item Two: The Swindle goes by many names,
Bribery and Theft, Fraud and Graft.
It's the dirty dealings among members of the Clan,
Who cheated who, or greased another's palm.
A yen for justice in the human breast
Inspires interest in each traitor or thief,
So ages after Cataline's plot shocked Rome,
The news is Watergate or Teapot Dome.

"Item Three: Disaster is two-faced:
One is natural—fire, flood and drought.
The other results from human error—
Airplane crashes and melting reactors.
For centuries the Clan has dreamed of comfort,
But wins it from an independent planet,
That's why there's as much news in ruin
As when the Tigris flooded Babylon.

"Item Four: Disease is Disaster's kin,
The difference is it's unheard and unseen.
Lurking in food and the surrounding air,
It stalks every member of the Clan.
For each the thought of losing good health
Is as dreadful as the thought of death,
Yet excitement over cancer or TB
Is the same as ancient fear of leprosy."

Without shortage of items, the voice continued:
Item Five concerned the triumphs of the Clan,
Its treaties, its new frontier in space,
For its members deem themselves a chosen race.
But at last I knew why news is so routine—
It's dictated by basic fears and longings—
So I've gone to skipping it now and then,
For it'll be the same in the year three thousand.

The Beltway

Who would have objected when planners claimed
It would end the burdens of travel,
No stopping and starting, no traffic jams,
The whole trip at speeds desirable?
So was this gigantic wheel of poured stone
Built to gird the city, coiling lanes
So smooth and broad that many thousands
Can at one time turn toward their end.

Once I was keen on this kind of travel
And got on by watching how the others came.
Then I'd merge to center, give a signal
And make my way out toward the fast lane.
And for years I used it, going to work
On one segment, each day out and back.
I thought my daily efforts certain to pay off,
For I'd chosen the most progressive course.

In time the beltway seemed to have a life,
I mean the way it kept renewing itself.
There'd be gangs working all night to add lanes,
And overpasses rising, the columns first—
And these would stand for months without platforms
Like the legs of some vast Colossus.
And always its roar filled the air around
As the countless travelers sent up a din.

Only later did I question where it led,
For I began to have problems with its signs:
As with other roads, these read north or west,
But can a circuit have a direction?
Then I remembered I'd not been all around,
And to see the thing, set out and returned,
And I'll admit that trip helped me understand
Some roads yield only motion without end.

The Lady

You've got to wonder if she knows what she's doing
Because she stands serenely in the harbor,
And tirelessly holding in her right arm
The torch she's burned for many years,
She graciously bids everyone to come.
Behind her beats the brain of the New World,
Thundering and smoking on the shoreline:
Up and down beat its vast ridges of concrete
And the lights wink on and off as it thinks
Of new ways of creating space.

You've got to wonder what she's been promising
And whether they feel at all deceived
As they come from Antigua or Pakistan—
Not just to New York—but to such cities
As Miami, Los Angeles, or Boston,
And first step onto shaking streets.
When their ears go numb from the traffic's din,
And buildings, like a canyon's cliffs,
Rise skyward to eclipse the firmament,
Do they think of the homeland they left?

You've got to ask one of them for directions
After a few years have brought city work.
As the answer comes in a tongue like your own—
Broken, mangled, and yet the common speech—
You'll realize the Lady is using them
To rebuild avenues beneath your feet:
Today the sinews in their shoulders and chests,
Tomorrow, minds of daughters and sons.
Even now they are schooled in the calculus
Which can stretch a skyscraper for space.

In return she plants a vision in their heads
Of a green lawn encircling a home,
On which without consent no foot may step,
And to encourage all, she makes it real for some.
This is the way it's been: after the English,
The Germans, the Irish, the Italians . . .
You've got to wonder how long it can last,
But don't presume: only the Lady knows,
And you might see from the set of lips and chin
That—like all ladies—she prizes discretion.

The Inns

They wait for him. The doors and windows looking,
The walls listening to the highway's wheels.
Maids are cleaning, barmen icing the wine,
In poolside gardens managers rehearse
The words which will make him feel most welcome,
But all are afraid he will not choose them.

They wait for him. Then the doors of the lobby
Open, and they see waiting was the right thing.
Clean-shaven, trim, suited up impeccably,
With unweathered face, neither old nor young,
He wheels to the desk with decisive bearing
And buys a key to his numbered room.

Later in the dining room they wait on him,
While in his mind a connection whirs,
Someone to deal with in the nearby town,
Someone to whom he'll make an offer.
He crafts his words until they make most real
Not what he's selling, but the fruits of the deal.

It's for him, he knows that, but thinks as he dines
How he'll be helping the buyer's family,
Helping the town, for even those serving him
Know better days when business succeeds.
All that's required is that they see reason,
Endorse growth and stifle fear of change.

Later on in the lounge they wait on him,
"Just like home," as they often declare.
But he likes it better, for here he finds
That by drawing his wallet he can lure
Friendly eyes and ears willing to listen,
And back home that takes effort and time.

Megalopolis

I

He felt no alarm over its dimensions,
Nor about the way it was growing.
It was enough for him to get around
And given a numbered point in its mass,
He could pick the most direct of lanes
And arrive there with dispatch.
He treated streets like intersecting lines,
The skyscrapers were their odds and evens,
And each of these, a vertical axis,
Traversed by numbered floors whose planes
Were sectioned by hallways into rooms.
The key to the plan was division.

He felt no alarm—until one afternoon
He drove to a favorite restaurant.
There was a block-long hole where it had been,
Filled with men and machines at work.
They were scraping and moving the earth around
While in mobile homes up on the street,
Architects were poring over the plans,
Coordinating each motion and effort.
They were bringing a grander building to being,
But the sight gave him cause to reflect:
If they could transform the city's brick and stone,
Suppose they thought of trying it on humans?

II

Oh city, your name is number.
    Your hundreds, thousands, millions
    Are boldly spoken out in steel and stone,
    To divide and to multiply—
    That is your vocation,
And you are rational: of zero you know nothing.

Oh city, as I enter you

You make so many of me
The exponential selves and sides appear,
Those who I have been
In Athens, New York, Rome,
Those who I will never be
Staring down
From a million vacant windows
The vacant eyes stare down.
And what conclusion should be drawn?

Oh artful city! Yours is a fertile brain,
    Commanding the sluggish hinterlands.
    Your nerve cords are tentacular—
    Rails, highways, shipping lanes,
    Woven through forests, seas, and mountains.
    You stretch beside them smaller fibres,
    Endless miles of wires on poles
    In which messages are coming and going,
    I can hear the voices bargaining,
    Promoting, setting prices,
    Calling in the cattle and the grain.

    I can hear the meters clicking
    And the registers ringing,
    Hear the rustling of shuffled papers,
    Hear you breaking your own records
    Every morning
As I enter you, oh my city.

III

After the pyramidal temple mounds,
After the walled towns with spiraling cathedrals,
Man fashioned the metropolitan city—an artifact
Of unprecedented complexity. Meanwhile,
The earth continued to circle the sun,
Moving sixty-seven thousand miles an hour,
While the sun, one of a hundred billion stars
In the Milky Way, circled the galaxy's hub,
Moving six hundred thousand miles an hour.

The Hearing

I. A Definition of Justice

Can you say, citizen, what has been enshrined
In courthouses across the land? Why they're built
Like temples in the middle of the towns,
The highest of them rising on Capitol Hill
To duplicate the columned Parthenon?
Do not say the constitution. It is merely a form
Written down in longhand, amendable,
Not responsible for the air of expectation,
Hanging in the courtroom when the judge
Walks in, hanging throughout the proceedings—
Not the constitution. It merely protects
An invisible which is more sovereign.
And what, oh citizen, if not your reason—
The mind of most of the men and women,
And it will dictate laws according to whim
Or find justice. *Oyez, oyez, oyez . . .*
God save the United States.

II. Cases with Commentaries

If you could not say, if you had forgotten,
Listen while I lengthen these lines,
Listen to what happened after the reforms
Of Hammurabi, Solon, and Justinian.
When the sun was in the zodiac's seventh sign,
We, the people of the United States
Did establish a Congress House in our Federal Town,
And send there councilors to distribute among us
The riches of the hinterlands. *Oyez, oyez . . .*
Give attention, for the Court is now sitting.

"Your Honor, the plaintiff, a boxer by profession,
Is unlettered, from an impoverished background,

36

But has used his talents, his arms and hands,
To knock from the ring many opponents.
After he pays promoters and tax collectors,
Is there a reason he should not keep
One-half the gate of his fight last year—
A figure of some ten million dollars?"

We, the people, ordain no act of Congress
Shall infringe our freedom to bring suit
Against one another, and to that end,
Have educated one million lawyers.
Outnumbering our scientists by ten times,
They are masters of courtroom debate,
And for a sum, will argue on offense or defense,
Regardless of the merits of the case.

"Your Honor, my client is a fine young man,
Who believes his father has wronged him,
By not providing money for his college education,
And causing him to have to go to work.
It is true the elder man, a carpenter by trade,
Has several small children still at home,
But is there a reason he could not have done more
Than provide eighteen years of food and shelter?"

If the son curseth the father, he shall
Surely be put to death. Thou shalt rise
Up before the hoary head.

In the United States the average citizen
Has yearly income twenty-five times greater
Than a person in Kenya or Pakistan—
And it buys him what the other dare not dream.

Thou shalt not see thy brother's ox go astray
And hide thyself from it . . . Thou mayest not
Hide thyself.

III. An Advisory Opinion

If I listen long enough
If I will only listen,
When my claim comes against my brother's,
If I look within and listen,
A form who shares our form
Decides which claim is more rightful.

I do not know where it comes from.
Do you know where it comes from?
At one time I thought it was learned.
That was because I did not listen
Because I had forgotten.
Now I think behind decision there lies
Imagination, offering up the possibilities,
To reason, which judges them, and selects.
But where do reason and imagination come from?

I do not know where they come from.
Can you say where?
Isn't the important thing the decision?
The first was in favor of the weak
Against the strong; from which the escape
From nature began, and the law,
Its long evolution.

But I am neither Solon nor Jefferson,
Am a citizen upon the middle ground,
Seeming always between good and base actions,
Between all of those who chose the right
Most of the time, and those who decided
In favor of the wrong,
Because they did not listen,
Because they have forgotten,
Because they would not listen long enough.

Elder

With your head start in darkness
You gave me sight,
Fire from whom I was lighted.
Here before, you warmed the way:
I burn now along your line.

But you are fainter, fitful and dim,
As you gutter and choke in your bed.
The darkness laps about your brain
As dying down, you shoot random sparks,
Mumble memories and broken songs.

Against the darkness I would build you up:
For a bit of heat, feed breath and bread.
For I would not burn naked into the cold,
Farther from the beginning,
And no light ahead.

Nobody

How then are you
Ever nimble,
Tripping down the stairs
Into this quiet room?

Do keep moving
One step more:
Now you stand still beside me,
Little fire with no flesh.

Then you vanish
On limbs of sleep
With your shy laughter,
Blue girl
Mood of mine.

Parrots

Maybe there were two of us all that time
I thought the voice my own,
Not one but two,
Each an echo to remind.
But who was following who?

Maybe the beak which must speak first
Says little about us,
What matters is that words begin
And between us reproduce
Until one tires of them.

And maybe we two can play on,
Finding diversion with tongues.
For pleasure we can change tempo,
And there's variety of tone,
One's high when the other's low.

Tale of the Hands

They have never forgotten the curved flanks,
The hills pressing their palms, as they ran
Rising and falling. And each day the same,
Like the feet, on and on, seeing only one thing.
So ages later, unsure of freedom,
They cannot hang in open air for long.

They have never forgotten, and return
When they open and grasp to fill the palms,
To handle coins, cloth, fruit, or other hands,
Before putting them down and pressing on.
And everything in the world is handsome,
So satisfaction eludes them.

They have never believed in the future,
Nor in any direction but their own;
Nor in the map which is sealed in their palms,
Telling how long they have with its lines,
Just how much of which century remains
Before the ship with all hands goes down.

Gaps

You'd better have your feet on pavement and steady nerves
When walking the street where you used to live,
And in the air of early spring you discover
Where your house stood, an empty lot stares.
And nearby men shovel asphalt on the street
To fill gaps opened by the ground beneath your feet.

The gaps wait patiently not to be here,
To clap empty hands, to give a warning stare,
To startle you who seem bent on forgetting
The houses enclose them, the streets cover earth
Which breathes them, freezing, thawing, heaving up
To ruin every structure hands have built.

And remember you are built around a gap,
Your chest and back are walls enclosing space,
And there breath comes to nourish arms and legs,
And for a time they are yours to direct.
Yet one day chest, limbs—all will come unbound
And leave you gaping at those who walk the town.

Scheme of Sky and Plain

In the west they are so open,
You would not expect deception:
Without a mountain the plain unfolds,
And lacks intrigue of dark woodlands,
Which might call forth suspicion.
And the sky's face is so open,
Despite its eye which shifts,
It never appears devious.

Yet you feel there is something
Sky and land will not make plain,
Some secret whispered all through the day;
It might concern seas which came between,
For the plain once held inland oceans.
The sky kissed it dry but clues remain:
In summer the flat plain brims with grain
And like ships farms float the grassy main.

More suspect is the place they meet,
As far away as they can reach,
Devising the line called horizon,
They conspire against your vision.
And like mariners of ancient times
You may wonder about their line:
Beyond it they might not exist,
There might be only endless emptiness.

Mountains

Confront them. They withhold the key.
Centuries are notes in their song:
From these humps came the idea of bison,
Grazing, shaking shaggy heads.

Knock. Their door is to be found,
Yet breath passes through this stone:
For they heaved up through astonished seas
To anchor the floating ground.

Listen. You might hear them as tongues,
Pointing toward heaven, speaking no age:
In words unconcerned as distant thunder,
They call: *Strong shoulder, strong shoulder.*

Ocean

Who cares about heaven
When you can bend its beams,
To brighten the skin of your back,
Then change your color
From blue-green to gray
In a light show lasting all day.

And what else are you doing,
Bent over, looking down,
With arms coiled around the shoreline
To squeeze up the dunes
And the ground where we stand
With a strength far beyond our ken.

Your wizardry would be alarming,
But for the peace you bring,
When your washing waves slide in
And breathe your name over and again,
The same syllables since time began,
An *ooshing* we say as ocean.

The Garden

Grr! There they are again!
Weeds all over the garden,
Shooting up, dangling, lolling:
Just after you hoe 'em
And think the work is done,
Like chaos they're reborn.

Damn! Can they spread ruin!
Horseweed, daisies, jimson,
Taking over everything:
After spreading roots around,
They are soon fingering
The necks of all your darlings.

Watch it! Don't take pity
On the weedy bloomers
With faces just like flowers:
They're worse than bad habits,
Spare that hoe a minute,
And soon you'll feel regret.

Potato

Bring the potato to plant beneath my feet,
Where it can swell in the earthen dark,
Pressed by the shades of those I love,
But with its eye on the world above.

Watch the potato sending green leaves
To drink secretly of the sun,
Transforming it into white sustenance
And sucking it down through a stem.

Watch the potato do its work above ground,
Disguised by many uses and names,
For the meal which Indians call *batata*
Becomes vodka, dye, paste, and starch.

Bring the potato as soup or chip,
I will eat it as do the Irish,
Whose bones fell down from want of it,
So the potato was the same as life.

Coffee

If one cup props eyelids up,
And gets you to coffee break,
Then you have two more at lunch,
The coffee is drinking you up.
But you need it for your wits,
Although it's not nutritious.
It gives you appetite for work
And makes the tongue alert.

Yet time comes for a golden mean,
And you find you'd cut anything,
Whether women, wine, or song,
Before broth from this bean.
So you watch as teeth grow stains,
And tongue turns a vivid green,
And wish that were the end of it,
When you think about your stomach!

The Bowl of Cereal

How do the flakes so calmly wait
There on my table looking up?
Don't they see my maw which gapes,
And which will grind them down to death
In the roiling pit of the stomach?

It may be they sleep and dream
Of how they spent last summer:
Then they crowned the fields of grain
And drank the wind and sunny air
Until they filled with pleasure.

Or they may summon quiet strength
From centuries of service:
From boards in history's first huts,
Where they began to do their best
Against great hunger's threat.

Cornfields: Late Summer

Some enemy must be making them stand
On guard like a national army.
Why else would they muster numbers so grand
And marshal them into battle lines?
Why else would they march up, growing strong,
First stalk, then sheath, then tassel,
Why fight off blights like smut and worms
Until they are taller than a man?
Some enemy must be threatening them.
Maybe their weapons are a clue.
For the spikes which point out from the hip
Will be transformed by wintertime
Into muscle and flesh and bone.

To the Rust

Do you know, rust, who you recall
With your mysterious hunger,
And the way you hide in atmosphere
With a maw which never appears?

Of our proudest metal you make meal:
The first course is air and water,
Then unseen jaws begin to tear,
And red scabs bloom everywhere.

Once underway, you return each day
To gnaw on the very same scabs,
Then in time the holes gape open—
Your smile of satisfaction.

But rust, your appetite for waste
Is steady and relentless,
So who is it you suggest,
Are you any kin to death?

Rivers

Travel one and see why a god was in it,
For what can it not carry on its back?
What freighted barges, fat yachts,
And craft bedecked with swimmers,
Can the river not bear without a bother?
So many humans has it borne to destinations,
In gratitude the towns press its flanks.

Listen to one and hear how human burdens
Were added to more ancient obligations,
For the river agreed with day as the world began
To take daylight upon its back at dawn,
Then to magnify it as the hours wore on.
This burden changes the river's skin color,
But it is rare to hear complaints above a murmur.

Live near one and learn its god-like tricks.
For the years seem to tame it in its banks,
Till you think that just beyond the house it passes,
When each day with quiet stealth the river sneaks:
Sliding in and rolling underneath your feet,
It picks you up and carries you—mortal cargo—
Toward a place where you have no wish to go.

Legs of Light, Torso of Darkness

The legs followed light, leaping straight up
Through the fire, then they were gone,
While in darkness the torso lying supine
And feeling the emptiness where they would be
Kept moaning: *There must be more of me.*

He never listened when they were one,
And never followed the light's direction.
For him to live was always enough,
Even though he knew that as he slept,
The smoke rose up from his flesh.

No wonder he doesn't want to wake up,
And thinks his days lack excitement.
No wonder that, immobile and flat,
All he can do is repeat vacantly:
There must be more of me.

The Plea

Please don't let the brief touch of that glance
Press your silent limbs into action,
Don't let its spell draw you down, like the tide,
Into that world where I can never come.
Time after time you have gone away,
Falling for strangers as if they were kin,
Citing needs (which are never my own),
For the music of laughter, for applause,
And each time you break your promise to stay.
Then all primeval differences return
And the curse of strife begins: alone,
With no one to hear what I am saying,
I watch you there, groping for the way.

On Friendship

You ask me why I have so few friends.
Well, alright, I'm going to tell you.
But let me first mention the one I do have—
He's never accepted me as I am:
The guy's just brimming with criticism
And so he's kind of hard to be around.

Of course, most times that's no problem,
He's never there when I need him:
He works from dawn to past midnight,
And usually straight through the weekend.
How does he account for such habits?
At the end, he says, he'll have time to rest.

You ask me why I have so few friends.
Well, the one I have is a man of learning,
And the times I do see him, he asks questions,
For which I spend entire days preparing.
Do I like Plato? Dante? Faulkner?
What about the astronomer, Kuiper?

So through him I've made other friends
Who make their own curious demands:
One claims that dancing and having fun
Mean little in the general scheme.
It's true these friends don't actually exist,
But their advice makes no less sense for that.

My friend insists that it deepens their worth
And to know them, he risks seeming boring,
But it's others who seem dull next to him,
For they lack his inwardness and depth.
If you still want to know why I have few friends,
Think how long it took to find this one.

Planning to Work the Weekend

I planned to work seven days in succession,
With no inkling of the trouble I'd bring on,
For each day I plotted a pile of work,
Then on Monday with the first I began.
Working hard as the weekdays rolled along,
I leveled the piles and checked them off,
I had unexpected problems with Thursday's stack,
But not enough to jeopardize my project.

It was on Friday the real trouble started.
The clock slowed, the work grew stubborn,
So at quitting time some was left
When the halls rang with laughter of friends.
Headed for Happy Hour, they trooped in
And asked me along. But when I spoke of work,
They looked at me with suspicion,
Then left me there to wonder what was wrong.

Feeling depressed, I finished the evening
And Saturday was on the job again.
But at mid-morning, my brother called up,
Offering to take me to the game.
Nothing's of more value than kin, he claimed,
And for work there's a time and a place.
When I still declined, his goodbye sounded hurt,
And undermined my appetite for work.

Two hours I hung on until my wife showed up,
Bringing lunch, but really hexing my plan:
She asked how I'd make it next week without rest,
Saying my whole face was drawn and wan.
When she left, I couldn't focus vision
And all importance ebbed from my plan.
I could see that to work the whole weekend
You'd have to be some kind of superman!

Of Homes and Men

House, I hate the way you would make me a man,
Always calling my hands to your form. You want
A painter to clothe you against northern winds,
A carpenter skillful with his tool,
A plumber to fix your pipes with his wrench,
For you are periodically dripping.

You want a man to worry on your flat white face,
As if suffering the dark windows stare.
No matter what repairs I've made,
No matter where or what I'm doing,
You make my mind wander, inspiring plans
Against time and theft and accident.

I hate it when you sing your siren-song,
Telling who I'll be as soon as I possess you.
Not once do you mention the cost of the bargain.
And I know you sing to a billion others
From cottages, colonials, ranchos, chateaus,
You sang from ancient huts of Asia Minor.

House, why don't you let me be myself,
Today, as the rains pour from heaven?
Pitch your roof like two hands folded in prayer
While I stretch out in a dark, quiet nook.
Be an ark anchored on a sea of grass,
And for a little while, give me some peace!

If Only

Like a Titan the day defies me,
Inert winter in cast iron color,
As we struggle I turn his ear
To the music of indecision,
To the question marks in the stark trees.

The contest never seems equal,
I can pin down a rock dead hand,
Press back the first of the freezing facts,
But one from another these ooze incessantly
From beneath his sodden skin.

I rotate his great bulk with care
As one would rotate a prism,
Search the crevices of moments for holds,
Strip off the calendar's furious page,
But naked, he is bigger than ever.

With no other choice I coax him,
Citing our common descent,
As I go I whisper in his own breath,
What could happen *if only* I say,
And repeat with persistence *if only*.

If he hears he gives not a sign.
Numerals bleed from the obese face,
And amazed by a gaze so blank,
I watch as his black shoes walk off
Again in their many directions.

Blizzard

Memory! How dry you become,
For you are there all night long,
Over and over your face returns,
Whitened and blank with obsession.

Is there a way through the pieces,
So countless nothing is clear,
You pile them high on every path,
Muffle footfalls, then fill the tracks.

And is there a point to the letter
You have pasted all over the ground?
Then why is it empty of all but a name,
Which the wheels write again and again?

So certain are you of revival,
You melt away and then return—
Out of the oceans, toward heaven drawn,
Your orbit girds the whole mind.

Wave

With you the heart swells
Till you are finally finished.
Oh, get up we say,
Your white mouth coming,
The things you would tell us—
So well traveled.

You bring in the bottles empty,
Your brittle wood, your sand
Your spun glass constellation.
Although it is always the same
In your age of water,
We never tire of hearing.

Your arrival starts an ancient clock,
The blind shells digging deep,
The birds beginning each time
Out and back like a prayer.

Your own track is left,
Although you do not sign it,
At the edge is your white name
Where you are curling forever.

Winter Leaves

But let the wings grow roots
and the roots fly.
                    —Juan Ramón Jiménez

When there are none, birds must do their work,
Weighing down the roots that would flap away.
By winter inverted into the soil of air,
The trees hold hungering bird-leaves.

When they were here, leaves stitched reversible
Clothes, to hang on limbs when they should fall.
The cloth was made of distance, so the limbs show,
But the birds get caught in the folds.

Yet even the bird-leaves flutter down
When hunger issues his order.
Then there is nothing but bare limbs
And the horizon, invitingly open.

Emanations

What the root sees is a light,
But he who steps downward measures his hope.

* * *

When you think that tides love them,
You wish that your arm was a fin.

* * *

Lamps are landmarks into distance, but to the sun
Strange ambition.

* * *

I sort and suck earth's sweetness. Too soon
I will return it.

The Saint

I can see how long now you will wait
With your blank open face
And the voice inside
Gathering in secret
For the next surprise
Like lightning through the ear.

And sure I will listen
As though we were kin:
We go separate ways,
We are all divided—
All but you who scarcely move:
It frightens me to think of your roots.

It must be your faith
Making me less than real,
For each time you begin
I am not my own:
A door opens and to my relief,
You have not become someone else.

The Hard Part

Wish, your wings are no longer becoming,
I will make you some feet for walking.
You should be two-legged and stand on your own,
With a face so you might be shown.
You must have weight, wish, so we will last,
You must remember the places we passed,
The road we traveled with you just in front,
Like my own shadow calling me on,
Making me see how large I have grown,
But how useless, unless you are known.